The Spiritual Expression of Friendship

Paramahansa Yogananda
(1893–1952)

The Spiritual Expression of Friendship

Paramahansa Yogananda

ABOUT THIS BOOK: *The Spiritual Expression of Friendship* features an essay, poem, and a poetic inspiration — composed by Paramahansa Yogananda in the early 1930s — on the ideals of true friendship and divine love. These writings originally appeared in early versions of the *Self-Realization Fellowship Lessons* and in *Self-Realization* magazine. Also included is the author's beautiful poem, "Friendship," which appears in his volume of poetry, *Songs of the Soul*.

First edition, 2025

Authorized by the International Publications Council of
SELF-REALIZATION FELLOWSHIP

The Self-Realization Fellowship name and emblem (shown above) appear on all SRF books, recordings, and other publications, assuring the reader that a work originates with the society established by Paramahansa Yogananda and faithfully conveys his teachings.

Library of Congress Cataloging-in-Publication Data

Names: Yogananda, Paramahansa, 1893-1952 author
Title: The spiritual expression of friendship / Paramahansa Yogananda.
Description: First edition. | [Los Angeles] : Self-Realization Fellowship, [2025] | Summary: "This book presents the teachings of Paramahansa Yogananda on the spiritual principles underlying human friendship, how to cultivate true, lasting friendships with others, and the benefits to be obtained through friendships based in spirituality"— Provided by publisher.
Identifiers: LCCN 2025008013 | ISBN 9781685682286 hardcover
Subjects: LCSH: Friendship—Religious aspects—Hinduism
Classification: LCC BL1215.F76 Y64 2025 | DDC 294.5/486762—dc23/eng/20250506
LC record available at https://lccn.loc.gov/2025008013

Printed in India

CONTENTS

PART I

PART II

Introduction

"Friendship is the highest form of love.... In friendship there is no compulsion; it is born of the free choice of the heart. It is God calling souls back to unity in Him. If you can be a friend to all, unconditionally, that is divine love."

—Paramahansa Yogananda

The ideal of true friendship is universally treasured, yet its higher purpose is not always recognized. In this book Paramahansa Yogananda, author of the spiritual classic *Autobiography of a Yogi,* reveals spiritual dimensions of friendship that are not commonly understood. He shows that when pursued in its purest and noblest form, friendship has the potential to take us beyond our ordinary everyday consciousness into an expanded, all-encompassing consciousness, wherein we feel a unifying divine kinship with others, and ultimately with all life. We come to experience the inclusive and embracing love that is the true nature of the soul.

A prolific writer and lecturer, Paramahansa Yogananda created a renowned and voluminous body of works on the yoga science of meditation and the art of balanced living. Whether speaking of finding the meaning and highest purpose of life, creating fulfilling relationships, raising spiritual children, overcoming self-defeating habits, or any of the other myriad goals and challenges of modern living, Paramahansa Yogananda continually refocuses our attention toward life's highest attainment: Self-realization — knowing our true nature as divine beings. We learn through the inspiration and encouragement of his teachings to live a truly victorious life by awakening to the infinite power and joy of our real Self: the soul.

It is our hope that this book will inspire you to look upon and develop your friendships in a new light. By practice of the principles presented herein and applying them to your various relationships, you will experience the upliftment that comes from the expression of true divine friendship, and the joy that comes from being a friend to all. In doing so, may you begin to perceive the One Friend hiding behind all friends, the Cosmic Love that is the source of all human love, and the Omnipresent Power that sustains all life.

SELF-REALIZATION FELLOWSHIP

Affirmation

By Paramahansa Yogananda

[Paramahansa Yogananda taught: "An affirmation should be repeated several times in succession during meditation, as well as several times during the day, with deep concentration and faith in its materialization, until it manifests as a reality in your life."*]

As I radiate love and goodwill to others, I will open the channel for God's love to come to me. Divine love is the magnet that draws to me all good.

* Complete instructions can be found in the author's *Scientific Healing Affirmations,* published by Self-Realization Fellowship.

Friendship

By Paramahansa Yogananda

Is friendship the weaving of the red strings
of two hearts?
Is it the blending of two minds into a spacious
one mind?
Is it the spouting of love founts together
To strengthen the rush of love on droughty souls?
Is it the one rose grown 'twixt twin mind-branchlets
Of one compassionate stem?
Is it the one thinking in two bodies?

Or is friendship like two strong stallions,
Disparate in color and mien,
Pulling the chariot of life together
To the one Goal, with one mind-sight?

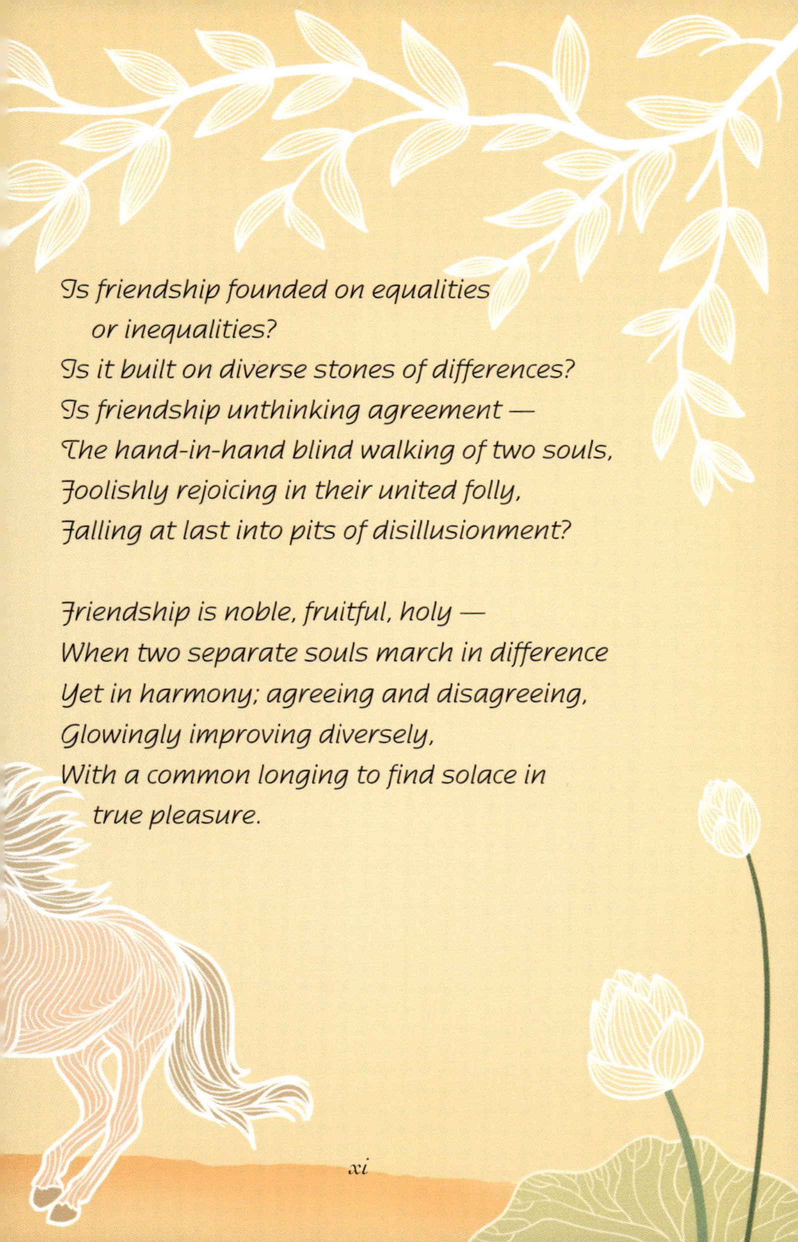

Is friendship founded on equalities
or inequalities?
Is it built on diverse stones of differences?
Is friendship unthinking agreement —
The hand-in-hand blind walking of two souls,
Foolishly rejoicing in their united folly,
Falling at last into pits of disillusionment?

Friendship is noble, fruitful, holy —
When two separate souls march in difference
Yet in harmony; agreeing and disagreeing,
Glowingly improving diversely,
With a common longing to find solace in
true pleasure.

When ne'er the lover seeks
Self-comfort at the cost of the one beloved,
Then, in that garden of selflessness,
Fragrant friendship perfectly flowers.
For friendship is a hybrid, born of two souls —
The blended fragrance of two unlike flowers
Blown together in love's caressing breeze.

Friendship is born from the very core
Of secret inexplicable likings.
Friendship is the fountain of true feelings.
It grows in both likeness and difference.
Friendship sleeps or dies in familiarity,
And decays in lusts of narrow-eyed selves.
Friendship grows tall and sturdy
In the soil of oneness in body, mind, and soul.

Demands, deceptions, sordid sense of possession,
Courtesy's lack, narrow self-love, suspicion,
Thoughtless, sharp-pointed, piercing words —
Cankers, these, which eat at the heart of
friendship.

Ah, friendship — flowering, heaven-born plant!
Nurtured art thou in the soil of measureless love,
In the seeking of soul progress together
By two who would smooth the way, each for
the other.
Watered art thou by attentions of affection
And the tender dews of inner and outer
sweetness
Of the selfless heart's inmost devotion.

Ah, friendship! where thy soul-born flowers fall,
There, on that sacred shrine of fragrance,
The Friend of all friends craves to come,
and to remain.

PART

I

THE SPIRITUAL EXPRESSION OF FRIENDSHIP

An essay written by Paramahansa Yogananda in the early 1930s

Part I

True Friendship Is a Universal Force That Reunites the Many With the One

Friendship is God's love shining through the eyes of your loved ones, calling you home to drink His nectar of eternal unity. Friendship is God's trumpet call, bidding the soul destroy the partitions of ego consciousness that separate it from all other souls and from Him. True friendship unites two souls so completely that they reflect the unity of Spirit and its divine qualities.

Friendship is the universal spiritual attraction that unites souls in the bond of divine love. It may manifest itself in the unity of two persons or of many. The Spirit originally was one. By the law of duality It became two: positive and negative. Then, by the law of infinity applied to the law of relativity, It became many. Now the One in the many is endeavoring to reunite the many into One. This effort of Spirit to unify many souls into One works through our emotions, intelligence, and intuition and finds its greatest expression through friendship.

Realize Your Kinship With All Humanity

True friendship is broad and inclusive. Selfish attachment to a single individual, excluding all others, inhibits the development of divine friendship. Gradually extend the boundaries of the glowing kingdom of your love to include your family, your neighbors, your community, your country, all countries — all living, sentient creatures. Be a cosmic friend, imbued with kindness and affection for all God's creation, sowing love everywhere. Such is the example set by the avatars and saints. Such has been the way of Jesus Christ, Lord Krishna, Swami Shankara,* St. Francis, and my great masters: Babaji, Lahiri Mahasaya, and Swami Sri Yukteswar.

Consider no one a stranger. Learn to feel that everybody is akin to you. Family love is merely one of the first exercises in the Divine Teacher's course in friendliness, intended to prepare your heart for all-inclusive divine love. Realize that the same lifeblood is circulating in the veins of all races. How may anyone dare to hate any other human being, of whatever race, when God lives

* Swami Shankara (Adi Shankaracharya), who lived in India in the late eighth or early ninth century A.D., reorganized the ancient monastic Swami Order. He is considered India's greatest philosopher.

and breathes in all? We are Americans or Indians or other nationalities for just a few years, but we are God's children forever. The soul cannot be confined within man-made boundaries. Its nationality is Spirit; its country is Omnipresence.

God's effort to unite strife-torn humanity manifests itself within each heart as the friendship instinct. It is not necessary to know and love all human beings and other creatures personally and individually. All you need do is to be ready at all times to shed the light of friendly service over all living creatures whom you happen to meet. This attitude requires constant mental effort and preparedness; in other words, unselfishness. The sun shines equally on diamond and charcoal, but the former has developed qualities that enable it to reflect the sunlight brilliantly, while the latter is unable to reflect the sunlight. Emulate the diamond in your dealings with people. Brightly reflect the light of God's love.

All this may seem very complicated, but when in deep meditation you touch the Infinite, your difficulties will melt away. Divine love will come to you. Beautiful intuitive experiences of universal friendliness will play like fountains in your mind.

Friendship Is Necessary to Evolve Human Consciousness Into Cosmic Consciousness

There are people who do not trust anyone, and who utterly doubt the possibility of ever having true friends. Some, in fact, actually boast that they get along without friends. But those who fail to be friendly disregard the divine law of Self-expansion, by which alone the soul evolves and returns to Spirit.

Those who fail to inspire confidence in other hearts, who are unable to extend the kingdom of their love and friendliness into other soul-territories, can never expand their consciousness into cosmic consciousness. If you cannot conquer human hearts, you cannot conquer the Cosmic Heart of God.

Real friendship is a manifestation of God's love for you, expressed through your friends. When perfect friendship exists either between two hearts or within a group of hearts (as in a spiritual organization), such friendship perfects each individual. The heart purified by friendship provides an open door to unity. Through it you should invite other souls to enter the temple of brotherhood — those who love you, and even those who love you not.

Mutual Service Is the Keynote of Friendship

To have friends, you must manifest friendliness. If you open the door to the magnetic power of friendship, souls of like vibrations will be attracted to you. The more friendly you become toward all, the greater will be the number of your real friends.

True friendship consists in being mutually useful. It means offering your friend good cheer in distress, sympathy in sorrow, advice in trouble, and material help in times of real need. Friendship consists in rejoicing in the good fortune of your friends and in sympathizing with them in adversity. One who has given his or her friendship to another gladly foregoes selfish pleasures or self-interest for the sake of that friend's happiness, without consciousness of loss or sacrifice, and without counting the cost.

Help your friends by being a mental,

aesthetic, and spiritual inspiration to them. Making others happy, through kindness of speech and sincerity of right advice, is a sign of true greatness. Never be sarcastic to a friend. To hurt another soul by sarcastic words, looks, or suggestions, is despicable. Sarcasm draws out the rebellious spirit and anger in wrongdoers. Loving suggestions bring out repentance in them. Repentance consists in thoroughly understanding one's own error and in abandoning it.

Friendship is pure by nature. When you have a lily in your hands, how can you crush it? When you love a person dearly, how can you want to give hurt, even though he or she may be wrong? Divine love is unlimited and infinite. When two or more persons are friends always, no matter what happens, that is an expression of divine love, or divine friendship.

Be True to Yourself and Others, and You Will Gain the Friendship of God

Do not flatter your friends, but encourage them with sincere praise. Do not agree with them when they are wrong. One who feels real friendship cannot witness with indifference a friend's indulgence in harmful pleasures. This does not mean one should pick a quarrel. Suggest mentally; or if your advice is asked, give it gently and lovingly. Fools argue; friends discuss their differences.

Avoid doing anything that brings harm to yourself or to another. If you are self-indulgent, or if you encourage a friend in ignoble vices, you are an enemy disguised as a friend. Be true to yourself and to others, and you will gain the friendship of God. Once you make your love felt in other people, it will expand until it becomes the one Cosmic Love that flows through all hearts.

Always remember that you need the

inspiration of better company — of those more highly evolved than yourself — to keep constantly improving. And you should also share your own goodness with people of inferior qualities who need your help. A saint once said: "Good company is of paramount importance, as it influences your reason and will, which, by repetitions of good thoughts and actions, form good habits." Your good thoughts and good habits formed by outer good company are your best *inner* friends.

Unfailing Laws of Friendship

Friendship should not be influenced by the relative positions of people. It may and should exist in all relationships: between lovers, employer and employee, teacher and pupil, parents and children, friend and friend.

Be neither unduly familiar with, nor indifferent to, a friend. Moreover, do not "trademark" any friend by assuming, "I know all about you." Respect and love grow among friends with time. "Familiarity breeds contempt" between those who are mutually useless, selfish, materially minded, and unproductive of inspiration or self-development. The greater the mutual service, the deeper the friendship. Why does Jesus have such a wide following? Because he, like other great masters and avatars, excelled in service to humanity. Hence, to attract friends, one must possess the qualities of a real friend.

Human love and friendship have their basis in service on the physical, or mental, or business plane; they are conditional and may be short-lived. Blind friendship between selfish and unthinking persons may end suddenly in blind hatred. Jealousy, for example, is self-love and death to friendship. But divine love has its foundation in service on the spiritual and intuitional planes, and is unconditional and everlasting. Only mutual effort to build wisdom and spiritual and intuitive understanding can bind two souls by the laws of everlasting, universal divine love.

Friendship Is the Basis of Marital Happiness

Unless conjugal love has a spiritual basis, it can never last. If husbands and wives are to live in friendship and harmony, they must be of spiritual service to each other. It is the newlyweds who forget that true (spiritual) love is based on unselfish mutual service and friendship who soon come to a parting of the ways. When two souls are ideally mated, their love becomes spiritualized and is registered in eternity after death as the one love of God.

Practice Loving Those Who Do Not Love You

It is easier to serve with divine love those persons who are in tune with you than those who are antagonistic to you. After you learn to serve lovingly those who are near to your heart, then learn to extend that love even to your enemies — first, from a distance; and then, if they respond, at close quarters by some personal gesture of love or friendship.

The secret of Christ's strength lay in his love for all, even his enemies. Far better to conquer by love the heart of individuals who hate you than to vanquish them by vindictive force. To ordinary persons such a doctrine seems absurd. Their first impulse is to return two slaps for the one they have received — and to add a kick for good measure!

Why should you love your enemies? In order that you may bring the healing rays of your love into their dark, hatred-stricken hearts. When friendship is so released, it can behold itself as pure golden love. Thus will the flame of your love burn away the partitions of hatred and misery that separate your soul from other souls and that separate all unenlightened souls from the vast sea of Infinite Love.

Practice loving those who do not love you. Feel for those who do not feel for you. Be generous to those who are generous only to themselves. Hatred is destructive to self and to others. If you heap hatred upon your enemies, neither they nor you will be able to perceive the inherent beauty of your soul.

If humility and apologies on your part will bring out the good qualities of persons who consider themselves your enemy, by all means apologize when necessary. The person who can do this has attained a definite spiritual development, for it takes character to be able to apologize graciously and sincerely. It is the consciousness of one's own inferiority that makes a person hide behind a display of pride. Do not, however, encourage a wrongdoer by being too humble and apologetic. You need not fawn on your enemies, just silently love them. Silently be of service to them whenever they are in need, for love is real only when it is useful and expresses itself through action. Thus you may rend the veils of hatred and of narrowmindedness that hide God from your sight.

You may ask: "How can I learn to love my enemies? I am not strong enough to do that." My answer is this: "Constant communion with the Infinite by Self-Realization Fellowship methods of meditation fills one with divine love, which alone enables one to love one's enemies."

Seek Friends of Past Incarnations and Perfect Your Friendship With Them

Make every effort to rediscover your friends of past incarnations, whom you may recognize through familiar physical, mental, and spiritual qualities. Rising above considerations of material or even spiritual gain, try to resume such friendships, begun in a preceding incarnation, and perfect them into divine friendship.

One may come in daily contact with some people and yet not feel in sympathy with them. You have to adapt yourself to such persons and learn to love them. But there are others with whom you feel instantaneously sympathetic at first meeting; it seems as though you have always known them. This indicates that they are your friends of previous incarnations. Do not neglect them, but strengthen the friendship existing between you. It is easier to cultivate the seeds of divine friendship on the soil of loving relationships from past incarnations than to try to grow friendship on the stony ground of hearts that are not in tune with yours.

Always be on the lookout for friends of past incarnations, by being calm within when you meet others. Mental restlessness and inattention may prevent your recognizing such friends. Not infrequently such old friends are very near you, drawn into the orbit of your life by the friendship born in the dim, distant past. They constitute your shining collection of soul-stars. Add to it constantly and seek in these bright galaxies to behold the one Great Friend smiling at you radiantly and clearly. It is God who comes to you in the guise of a true and noble friend to serve, inspire, and guide you.

All human beings have their own conception of what constitutes physical and mental beauty. What seems ugly to one may appear beautiful to another. Looking at a crowd, you like some faces instantly; others do not attract you. The immediate attraction of your mind to the inner and outer features of an individual is your first indication that you have found a friend of the past. Your dear ones whom you loved before are drawn toward you by a prenatal sense of friendship.

Do not be deceived by physical beauty. Ask yourself whether or not the expression of a face, the manner of walking, everything about a particular person appeals to you. Sometimes overeating and lack of exercise may sufficiently change the features of a friend of former lives so that he or she escapes your recognition. But an unattractive body may harbor the soul of a real friend. Sometimes a beautiful woman falls in love with a homely man, or a handsome man with a physically plain woman, owing to the loving friendship of a past incarnation.

Therefore, to be sure that your eyes have not deceived you with regard to physical characteristics of a person whom you surmise may be a former friend, ascertain whether you are mentally and spiritually congenial. Guard yourself against being prejudiced by little peculiarities. Delve deeply into that person's mind in order to find out whether your tastes and inclinations essentially agree. Seek your friends of past incarnations in order that you may continue your friendship with them in this life, and perfect it into divine friendship. One lifetime is not always sufficient to achieve the perfection of unconditional divine love between friends.

Ugliness of disposition and selfishness drive away all friends of former incarnations, whereas friendliness draws them toward you. Therefore be ready always to meet them halfway. Never mind if one or two friends prove false and deceive you, for others that are true will bring you many blessings.

Keep in mind this prayer:

> "O Divine Friend, let those who are my own come unto me. Finding them, may I perfect our friendship, and find friendship with all; thus may I find Thee."

The Ennobling Effects of Friendship Expand the Consciousness of Each Individual

When true friendship exists between two souls and they seek spiritual love and God's love together, when their only wish is to be of service to each other, their friendship produces the flame of Spirit. Through perfected divine friendship, mutually seeking spiritual perfection, they find the one Great Friend.

When divine friendship reigns supreme in the temple of your heart, your soul will merge with the vast Cosmic Soul, bursting the confining bonds that separated it from all of God's animate and inanimate creation.

When you behold — assembled all at once beneath the canopy of your perfected universal friendship — the souls of the past, present, and future, then the friendship thirst of your heart will be quenched forever. Feel the love that unites the busy stars, the amoeba, the whippoorwill, the nightingale, the dumb stones, the shining sea sands. Then God's creation will ring with the emancipating song of all-difference-dissolving celestial friendship. Then the Divine Friend will rejoice to see you come Home after your evolutional wanderings and roamings through the pathways of incarnations. Then He and you will merge in the bliss of eternal friendship.

An Affirmation to Practice

Today I will forgive all who have ever offended me, and I will give my love to all thirsty hearts — both to those who love me and to those who do not love me.

PART

II

Love Is the Breath of Spirit

A poetic inspiration penned by Paramahansa Yogananda in the early 1930s

Part II

Many are the seekers of love, but few know what love is or how it is to be found. Love is the invisible reservoir of joy flowing out of the heart of the Infinite into the channels of human souls and all things. Love is joy in the true joy of others.

Love is born in the cradle of spontaneous mutual liking. It may be found roaming in parental, filial, friendly, conjugal relations; yet its home is the sacred temple of a pure heart, where it dwells unconditioned by limitations of compulsive instincts or sensual gratifications. Love reigns on the throne of unselfish respect for other souls. Love expires when selfishness stabs its soul.

Part II

Love awakes in aesthetic, intellectual, emotional, social, religious, psychological, metaphysical, material, marital, and spiritual usefulness of one soul to another or to others. Love sleeps in indifference, wrong familiarity, discourtesy, soul-stabbing words, and the change of death.

Part II

Demons of passion, attachment, and superficial likings born of sense attraction have disguised themselves in the cloak of love and have devoured the hopes of many. But as light cannot be called darkness, so nothing can make love evil. Love is pure, wherever it truly exists. Love can be hidden or obscured, but never desecrated; for its divine nature abides in the inviolable innermost sanctum of the soul.

PART II

Love is the breath of Spirit. It is the heartbeat of God, throbbing in aught that exists, animate or inanimate. Love is the queen, wisdom is the king, and all things are their offspring. The queen is the harmony that rules the cosmos, and the equilibrium that keeps the island universes and planetary systems in balance. Without the attraction of love, God could not coax wandering forces to join the symmetrical dance of cosmic creation, nor hold will-endowed souls in the shelter of law and harmony.

Part II

Love is the music from the flute of eternity. Love is the wail of the viol of wisdom. Love is the echo of Spirit reverberating through souls, urging them to return Home — hands clasped, minds clasped, lives clasped, souls clasped in the succor of collective usefulness of cooperation.

Part II

Love blooms in the complete mutual exchange of noble virtues. It is the fragrance of the blossoms of all sweet qualities bound together in a redolent bouquet. That bouquet of love is the consummate gift to the Father-Mother-Friend-Beloved of all. The offering of perfected love is the passport required of each soul to enter heaven.

Part II

Love is the ocean of eternal unity, where the meandering rivers of all little lives are to merge into the resplendent vastness of blissful, immortal Spirit.

About the Author

Paramahansa Yogananda (1893–1952) is widely regarded as one of the preeminent spiritual figures of our time. Born in northern India, he came to the United States in 1920, where for more than thirty years he taught India's ancient science of meditation and the art of balanced spiritual living. Through his acclaimed life story, *Autobiography of a Yogi,* and his numerous other books, Paramahansa Yogananda has introduced millions of readers to the perennial wisdom of the East. Today, his spiritual and humanitarian work is carried on by Self-Realization Fellowship, the international society he founded in 1920 to disseminate his teachings worldwide. The current president and spiritual head of Self-Realization Fellowship is Brother Chidananda.

An award-winning documentary film about Paramahansa Yogananda's life and work, *Awake: The Life of Yogananda,* was released in 2014.

Additional Resources on the Kriya Yoga Teachings of Paramahansa Yogananda

Self-Realization Fellowship is dedicated to freely assisting seekers worldwide. For information regarding our annual series of public lectures and classes, meditation and inspirational services at our temples and centers around the world, a schedule of retreats, and other activities, we invite you to visit our website or our International Headquarters:

www.yogananda.org

Self-Realization Fellowship
3880 San Rafael Avenue
Los Angeles, CA 90065
(323) 225-2471

Self-Realization Fellowship Lessons

Personal guidance and instruction from Paramahansa Yogananda on the techniques of yoga meditation and principles of spiritual living

If you feel drawn to the spiritual truths described in *The Spiritual Expression of Friendship,* we invite you to enroll in the *Self-Realization Fellowship Lessons.*

Paramahansa Yogananda originated this home-study series to provide sincere seekers the opportunity to learn and practice the ancient yoga meditation techniques that he brought to the West — including the science of Kriya Yoga. The *Lessons* also present his practical guidance for attaining balanced physical, mental, and spiritual well-being.

The *Self-Realization Fellowship Lessons* are available at a nominal fee (to cover printing and postage costs). All students are freely given personal guidance in their practice by Self-Realization Fellowship monks and nuns.

For more information...

Please visit www.srflessons.org to request a

comprehensive complimentary information packet about the *Lessons,* which includes:

- *"An Overview of the Self-Realization Fellowship Lessons: Information About Paramahansa Yogananda's Home-Study Series"*
- *"Highest Achievements Through Self-Realization," by Paramahansa Yogananda — a thorough introduction to the teachings presented in the SRF Lessons*

Also published by Self-Realization Fellowship...

Autobiography of a Yogi
by Paramahansa Yogananda

This acclaimed autobiography is at once a riveting account of an extraordinary life and a penetrating and unforgettable look at the ultimate mysteries of human existence. Hailed as a landmark work of spiritual literature when it first appeared in print, it remains one of the most widely read and respected books ever published on the wisdom of the East.

With engaging candor, eloquence, and wit, Paramahansa Yogananda narrates the inspiring chronicle of his life — the experiences of his remarkable childhood, encounters with many saints and sages during his youthful search throughout India for an illumined teacher, ten years of training in the hermitage of a revered yoga master, and the thirty years that he lived and taught in America. He records as well his meetings with Mahatma Gandhi, Rabindranath Tagore, Luther Burbank, the Catholic stigmatist Therese Neumann, and other celebrated spiritual personalities of East and West. Also included is extensive material that he added after the first edition came out in 1946, with a final chapter on the closing years of his life.

Considered a modern spiritual classic, *Autobiography of a Yogi* offers a profound introduction to the ancient science of Yoga. It has been translated into many languages and is widely used in college and university courses. A perennial best seller, the book has found its way into the hearts of millions of readers around the world.

"A rare account." — The New York Times

"A fascinating and clearly annotated study." — Newsweek

"There has been nothing before, written in English or in any other European language, like this presentation of Yoga."
— Columbia University Press

Other Books by Paramahansa Yogananda

Available at bookstores or online at www.srfbooks.org

Autobiography of a Yogi

Autobiography of a Yogi *(Audiobook, read by Sir Ben Kingsley)*

God Talks With Arjuna: The Bhagavad Gita (A New Translation and Commentary)

The Second Coming of Christ: The Resurrection of the Christ Within You (A Revelatory Commentary on the Original Teachings of Jesus)

The Collected Talks and Essays
Volume I: Man's Eternal Quest
Volume II: The Divine Romance
Volume III: Journey to Self-realization
Volume IV: Solving the Mystery of Life

Wine of the Mystic: The Rubaiyat of Omar Khayyam — A Spiritual Interpretation

The Yoga of Jesus

The Yoga of the Bhagavad Gita

The Science of Religion

Whispers from Eternity

Songs of the Soul

Sayings of Paramahansa Yogananda

Scientific Healing Affirmations

Where There Is Light:
Insight and Inspiration for Meeting Life's Challenges

In the Sanctuary of the Soul: A Guide to Effective Prayer

How You Can Talk With God

Metaphysical Meditations

The Law of Success

Cosmic Chants

DVD VIDEO
Awake: The Life of Yogananda
A film by CounterPoint Films

A complete catalog of books and audio/video recordings — including rare archival recordings of Paramahansa Yogananda — is available on request or online at www.srfbooks.org.

SELF-REALIZATION FELLOWSHIP
3880 San Rafael Avenue • Los Angeles, CA 90065-3219
TEL (323) 225-2471 • FAX (323) 225-5088
www.yogananda.org